Life in Cut Time

Time Management for
Music Teachers

Emily Schwartz

To music teachers everywhere, from the marching band ladder to the conductor's podium; from the kindergarten singing circle to the college classroom. Thank you for making a difference.

CONTENTS

ACKNOWLEDGMENTS

This book would not have been possible without the help of some very special people. First and foremost, my amazing husband Dan, who is my sounding board, cheerleader, best friend, and daily inspiration. Also to my supportive family who always encouraged me to pursue my love of music. Huge thanks to my mom, who I can always count on to be a helpful editor. Thank you to all of the music teachers who have helped shape my life, including all of the music education faculty at the University of Southern California and Arizona State University, who consistently challenged my thinking and helped me grow into a better teacher. Thank you to Mesa Public Schools for giving me my first teaching job. You gave me so much more than a paycheck; you gave me a space to flourish and establish a career I love. Lastly, I'd like to thank my students. Thank you for reminding me every day why I love education.

1

LIFE IN CUT TIME

"Mom, when I grow up, I want to fill out lots and lots of paperwork." I am waiting to meet the child whose dream it is to get lost in a mountain of voicemails, paperwork, meetings, and parent teacher conferences. I know I certainly never envisioned my life like that. I knew from my first day of high school marching band that I wanted to be a music teacher; I loved music so much that I wanted to make sure it would never leave my life. It baffled me that my band director did not come skipping and smiling into the room at 6:35a.m. every morning like I did.

"You get to be a band geek all day long and get *paid* for it," I used to think. "What better profession could there possibly be?"

For sure, there were plenty of people lined up to burst my bubble about music teaching, but I didn't listen to them. "Be careful!" they used to say. "Teaching is great, but the extra 'stuff' can really bog you down."

"Be careful," my college professors told me. "You think the biggest challenge you'll face your first year will be remembering trill fingerings on the clarinet, but it will really be time management."

This didn't phase me because, you see, I knew *everything* back then (as most college freshmen do) and I knew I could handle all of the "stuff" teaching could throw at me.

"Teaching is going to be great! I'm going to change children's lives! I'm going to have the top program in the state! The most efficient classroom you've ever seen! I'll meet the standards, contact each parent weekly and be at a different competition every weekend."

Fast-forward four years, to the first month of my first year of teaching beginning band. Day 17 to be exact:

I'm sitting at my desk, exhausted, peeking over a stack of four or five clarinets that need repairing and multiple school-policy handbooks to read. I'm trying to remember how to check my voicemail that surely has a bazillion messages from parents asking why the concert hasn't been scheduled yet. I quickly realize, however, that the pursuit of my voicemail pin number will have to be postponed yet again, for I am late to a mandatory in-service about how to use a document camera. (The best part of that story is that I don't even *have* a document camera in my room.)

This job wasn't anything close to what I imagined my first job would be. I thought I would teach high school marching band and here I was teaching elementary general music half the day and beginning band for the other half. Clarinet trill fingerings? Forget that! My biggest pedagogical question thus far in my teaching career was how to get 5-year-olds to sit down in a circle without either of us crying.

I remember closing my eyes tightly in hopes that when I opened them again, all of this "stuff" would go away and I could just get started being the music teacher I wanted to be.

My "first month of school" story is not unique by any means. It is practically a rite of passage that all music teachers must experience so they have something to talk about at Happy Hour on Fridays. However, while some of the initial shock disappears after the first year, the overflow of "stuff" that comes with teaching never really goes away.

Just when you think you have it figured out, something changes. All of a sudden, you're teaching guitar! Or you have moved to block scheduling! Or your principal says, "Gee, it'd sure be nice if we had a school musical. Would you direct one?" (We all know the words "would you" in that last sentence might as well not be there.) All of these extra tasks dropped in our schedules can add up to a giant time management nightmare.

On a recent flight home, I mentioned to the man sitting next to me that I was writing a time management book for music teachers. He paused and replied with a puzzled look on his face.

"I have a deep respect for teachers," he said cautiously, "but why do they struggle with time management? It seems that their whole day is already scripted out for them."

I couldn't help but chuckle. "Where do I even begin?" I thought to myself. Sure, our day is scripted out with a class schedule. That is the time we actually spend at the front of the classroom engaged with students. That's the "teaching" part. As soon as those students leave our rooms, we have mountains of work to do in order to prepare to come back and teach them again the next day. We have performances to plan, report cards to fill out, parents to call and meetings to attend. We are usually given prep time during the day to take care of some of these things, but all it takes is one student discipline problem or one last-minute administrator meeting to wipe out that time for the day.

Music teachers frequently find themselves with two days worth of work and half a day to complete it.

This is why it feels like we live in cut time.

So how do we slow down? How do we bring our teaching jobs back into a less stressful tempo?

Teachers have to think about time management differently than other professionals. In other professions there are more opportunities to delegate to colleagues and more flexibility in deciding when certain tasks should be completed. Music teachers on the other hand are often part of a very small department at the school and have zero flexibility over when they get a bathroom break, much less over when they can fit their work in. This is why some of the "traditional" time management advice out there doesn't always work for teachers. Our problem is finding balance in our day. I find it helpful to think about time management in teaching the same way you'd think about eating a balanced diet.

The Time Diet

We wouldn't eat only steak one week and then nothing but carrots another week and expect to feel healthy or energetic. You need to eat a balanced selection of food groups to stay healthy. Similarly, this sense of balance needs to apply to our workday, but we as teachers hardly ever do that. Instead, we run ourselves ragged because we care so much about our students. In order to get that balance back in your day and reduce your stress level, you need to put yourself on a Time Diet.

Think about all of the non-teaching things you do during the day. They are all important or you wouldn't be doing them, but are they all equally difficult? No! That is why every task you do as a teacher belongs to a different "food group."

1. Meats

These are difficult tasks that take a lot of thinking. Some common examples include things like score preparation, lesson planning, maintaining parent communication, etc...

2. Vegetables

These tasks are still important, but aren't as difficult to complete. Some common Vegetable tasks for music teachers are filing, grading, completing inventories, ordering supplies or attending meetings.

3. Desserts

Desserts are our fun things. These are the times we get to converse with our co-workers, bask in the glow of a finished concert or enjoy the rewards of teaching.

The trick to having excellent time management skills as a music teacher is to have a "balanced diet" of tasks each day. The problem is that we don't naturally do this. If left to our own devices, music teachers will do three things:

1. Clump all of the Meat tasks together

2. Become frustrated and bogged down with the Vegetables

3. Never make time to focus on and enjoy Desserts

These three factors quickly lead to burnout. See if this scenario sounds at all familiar:

It's the final few weeks of the semester. Your voicemail light is blinking, as it has been for the past week or so. You know that one of those messages is from your school secretary reminding you that you haven't input grades yet, but since you've successfully avoided her in the office, you're fairly certain you can keep her at bay for another 24 hours. You're pretty sure you once had a desk in your room, but it's now covered in student permission slips for the upcoming field trip. You haven't ordered buses yet. That was on the plan for today, but you spent your 30-minute lunch break documenting the fight you broke up in the hall after 1st period. The Teachers' Lounge? Does that place exist anymore?

We've all had weeks like this, but the more we can do to prevent them the better. Few of us *like* dieting, but sometimes it is the only way. The above scenario is filled with extra workday "fat" and stress that we must eliminate. Of course we're always going to have weeks that are more of a challenge than others, but that doesn't mean we can't do everything possible to minimize them and the negative effect they have on us.

Teachers are constantly asked to do more with fewer resources. The decreasing resource that gets the most attention is money, but an equally important one is time. While I know you had classes in music history, instrumental methods and music theory in college, I'm sure you *didn't* have "Time Management 101." It's not too late.

The following chapters contain ten strategies for you to use in your teaching to help put yourself on a Time Diet and bring a sense of balance back into your day. Your stress level will thank you. Teachers, say goodbye to your "Life in Cut Time."

2

YOUR PERFORMANCE IS ONLY AS GOOD AS YOUR WARM UP

"Sarah, please go grab clarinet #14 off the shelf. That will be your instrument for the year."

When I gave this simple instruction to a new fifth grade band student during my first experience with school-instrument checkout, I was making two very big assumptions:

1. Sarah knew what a clarinet case looked like.

2. Sarah was able to travel the ten feet back to her chair without opening the clarinet case.

I was wrong on both counts. That was just the beginning.

After quickly realizing that my instrument cabinet was little more than a fancy game of Tetris to my students, I knew the next steps I had planned would be a disaster. Once everyone was finally seated, I passed out the loan agreement forms. These forms had carefully and clearly labeled lines on which students would write information such as name, instrument and serial number. I thought they would need about five minutes to fill these out.

Once again, I was wrong.

"Do I fill out this line?"

"What kind of instrument is this?"

"What's a serial number?"

"Why are we doing this?"

"Hey! He stole my pencil!"

We didn't have enough time to finish the process during our 30-minute class. Instead, I was left with a bunch of disorganized instruments, half-completed loan forms, and no idea who went home with what.

Not only did this ruin the current day's plan, but it had a significant impact on the rest of the year's organization as well. After that first day, I never really had time to get caught up with my inventory; it was all I could do to keep up with the day-to-day demands of teaching. I never got around to regrouping and making sure all the instruments were accounted for.

This, of course, made a mountain of extra work and doubled my stress during the year as I tried to keep track of instruments with students transferring schools and equipment needing repair.

If I had only taken the time to get the instrument checkout process organized *before* the year started, I would have saved myself a lot of time and headache. But...it was summer then! I didn't want to start working yet and besides, I believed the same myth that many new teachers tell themselves: "I don't even know who my students are yet! Once I meet them, I'll have a better idea what their needs are and this will all be easier."

Strategy: Get as Much Done Before the First Day as Possible

Little did I know that once those students arrived, they would absorb all of my time. If I didn't *start* the year organized before the first student set foot in my classroom, I would be playing catch up until next summer.

It's tempting for veteran teachers to read my story and chuckle at the naïveté of a first-year-teacher, but experienced educators make these same mistakes too. We say, "Ugh, I have to make better use of those first few contract days next year!" But then next year comes and...well...we don't.

Your Year Needs a Warm Up

You would never send your students out on stage for a concert without first playing through some scales, long tones, or exercises. Those few minutes of warm-up are crucial to the success of the performance. They get everyone tuned, breathing correctly, and playing together. Students may groan when we begin the warm-up, (after-all, scales aren't the most exciting things in the world) but we insist that it's good for them.

The same is true for your school year. While the transition from summer to school is hectic and always creeps up on us, we need to take the time to "warm-up" by getting organized.

As music teachers, we rely heavily on our abilities to get large amounts of students to do one thing at the same time. That only happens with detailed and organized processes. However, these processes take time to implement. Those last few days of summer before the students arrive are golden and need to be maximized.

This is sometimes easier said than done because we are pulled in so many directions with Back to School Night, teacher meetings, and other such obligations. A little extra time in the beginning will save you loads of stress during the year.

After looking back at my botched instrument checkout experience, I changed many things about the process the following year:

I had each and every loan form pre-filled out with as much information as possible. I then circled the remaining areas students would need to fill in. Each form was placed inside its corresponding case. Each case was clearly labeled with the instrument name and number and placed in a designated area of the room. This all took time to set up, but I did it before the students arrived. The result made the work all worthwhile. The checkout went extremely smoothly. All students got their instruments, everything was organized, and I saved myself a lot of time and stress during the school year.

Take a moment to think of all of the things that need to be done or organized during the school year. What can you do ahead of time that will make the year go more smoothly?

A few suggestions:

1. Order music and organize the music library so everything can be found easily.

2. Set concert and event dates.

3. Write parent letters.

4. Prepare seating charts and grade books.

5. Have several days of sub plans in place.

6. Compile a list of frequently used phone numbers.

7. Complete supply orders.

8. Correspond with feeder schools.

9. Set up fundraisers.

10. Catalogue uniforms, music folders or other equipment that needs to be checked out.

Knowing Your Students

What about the legitimate concern new teachers have about not knowing their students yet? There is definitely merit to the fear that their prep work will be wasted because the prepared materials don't match the needs of their students.

This doesn't apply exclusively to new teachers. It applies to *any* teacher meeting *any* student for the first time.

It is important to utilize all resources available to find out as much as you can about your students before they arrive in order to minimize wasted time.

Strategies to find out student information:

1. Consult the previous music teacher

If you're in a new position, hopefully you're lucky enough to have contact with the previous teacher. Find out what procedures are already in place, what the students know, and any other pertinent information your predecessor can provide. If the previous teacher is unavailable, try other teachers in the district or even the school administrator.

2. Talk to your feeders

If you are in a secondary school position, keep regular contact with your feeder schools to get a good feel for what the needs of your students will be. Maintaining these relationships takes time, but just think of it as an investment that will pay off later.

3. *Meet with the students*

If your schedule and circumstances permit, hold a "get-to-know-you" meeting with students and parents before school starts. This allows you to get those introductions out of the way and get a head start on your organization so you can hit the ground running when the school year officially starts. If the only reason you don't meet with new students before the year starts is because "it's never been done before," give it a try!

Plan for Replication

As a teacher, you will find yourself needing the same materials at the same time year after year. Use this to your advantage! Taking time to re-create materials year after year not only wastes your time but also wastes your energy. "Re-creating things you've already done" doesn't even belong to one of the food groups in The Time Diet we talked about in Chapter 1. This wasted time is fat that has no place in your schedule.

As you prepare for the beginning of the year, ask yourself: "Is there a way I can make this easier on myself next year?"

After my first chaotic experience with instrument distribution, I wised up and dedicated time in the beginning of the school year to get organized. Even so, it still seemed to take *forever.* I realized I was printing out and writing down the same information over and over as I prepared the instruments for my students.

My husband was helping me with this and asked, "Why don't you merge all of your inventory information onto labels and just use those? Then you can stick one on the loan form, one on the instrument, and heck, you could even stick one on the kid! You'd have the file all ready to go for next year too."

Brilliant! Little things like that can streamline a process and save time.

Other ways to make replication easier:

1. Create checklists and written procedures for events

Keeping a written record of what you need for an event or a process to run smoothly can save you time and reduce your stress level. For example, if you plan to use the same fundraising company next year, keep the contact information in a folder on your computer along with any parent letters you might have sent home. Then, when it's time to do that fundraiser again, you won't have to spend your valuable time re-gathering and re-creating that information.

The first time you complete a process that requires a lot of "district red tape," such as taking the students on a field trip, it can be like navigating a complex maze of paperwork. (I'm convinced that this is some sort of new-teacher-hazing to make sure we can handle the job!) After you finally figure it out, you may promise yourself you'll remember the process next year, but odds are, you won't. Instead, as you fill out and gather the forms, save a copy in a folder complete with a quick note to yourself reminding you *who* needs *which* piece of paper. This will make the process much easier and faster next time.

2. Laminate

It is a well-known fact among teachers that every piece of paper a student touches disintegrates immediately. As you are preparing to start the year, if you run across an item you want students to use repeatedly throughout the year, run it through the laminator first. This way, you'll only have to copy it *once* and it will have a much better chance of standing up to your students' wear and tear. This also applies to posters or papers that you want to hang on your wall.

3. Communicate with parents efficiently

Part of being a good teacher, regardless of the subject you teach, is being a good communicator. Teachers complain that this takes up a lot of their time, but it doesn't need to. Every time you write a parent letter, save it in a folder on your computer for next year. Chances are, the information won't change drastically from year to year so all you'll have to do next time is change the date and edit a few details.

Calling parents on the phone takes more time than sending home a quick note. While calling is important, sending notes and emails home can be a faster and more efficient way of communicating on a more regular basis. Take a few extra minutes in the beginning of the year to compile parent email addresses into a mailing list. This will make communication much faster. Also, consider printing up a stack of note cards to set by your desk so you can quickly jot a note home to a parent about a student's progress. Making communication easy and fast not only saves you time, but increases the likelihood you'll actually do it!

4. Create templates

Any kind of document you create on a regular basis should have a template. This includes concert programs, rooming lists, requests for purchase orders, report cards, etc...Starting from scratch each time is wasteful and has no place in your Time Diet. Instead, the first time you create a new document, save it in a place that is easy to find, then use the "Save As" function on your computer to make a new one for the next year.

Don't Reinvent The Wheel

Music teachers are known for having a bit of a "super human" complex from time to time. Don't we always want to do everything ourselves? While this is a noble idea, it just isn't practical in terms of time management! Many music teachers before you have tried, (with success and failure) a number of different teaching methods. Use their experience to your benefit.

If you find yourself in a new teaching situation, whether it's your very first job or a new class you're taking on, don't insist on doing it all yourself! Seek out resources. Find out what's been done in the past. Talk to other teachers who have done the same thing. There is no shame in borrowing an idea from someone else. Teachers are in the business of helping people and that extends beyond their students. Never in my life have I met a music teacher who was unwilling to share ideas or resources with other teachers.

Last year, my school district needed to develop a music technology class. In order to increase enrollment in our district music program, the music supervisor thought of offering a class at the junior high level for students who might be more interested in a modern music technology class than traditional music ensembles. This sounded like a great idea, until a few teachers actually sat down and tried to imagine what this class would look like. We had no idea! None of us had ever been involved in a music technology class. We were starting from scratch.

If we had tried to do this by ourselves, it would have been a daunting task and I'm convinced it would never have materialized. Instead, we brought in an expert from the local university. We sought out other music technology programs to see what they offered. We also turned to music technology companies for advice on which equipment to purchase and for help in getting a package deal. It would have taken much longer for us to gather all of this knowledge on our own. We built on what others had already done and created something of our own with minimal time wasted.

Don't just seek help on the big important Meat tasks (like creating an entire curriculum.) Getting help on the little day-to-day Vegetable tasks is just as important. You're not the only one who has ever written a parent handbook or designed music t-shirts. You needn't reinvent the wheel. If the previous music teacher had something he or she was using, go with it! You may find that you'll want to add a few of your own personal touches later, but in the mean time, save your time and energy by borrowing.

Review

Starting the year off organized is essential to your time management. This means getting as much done before the students arrive as possible.

1. Know your students. Use your resources to find out about new students before they arrive so you can prepare accordingly.

2. Plan for replication. As you prepare procedures and materials, ask yourself, "What can I do now that will make this easier next year?"

3. Don't reinvent the wheel. Whatever resource you need, you're probably not the first person to need it. Be eager to ask others for help! One day soon, others may come to *you* for advice.

It is impossible to foresee every single thing you'll need in the beginning of the year, but taking the time to prepare what you can now will save you tons of time and stress later.

Life in Cut Time

3

GRACE NOTES ARE IMPORTANT TOO

Brandon was the kind of student who made teachers cringe when they saw him on their rosters. This student had been a menace to the school since his early days of kindergarten. He refused to work. Ever. He instead preferred to throw paper clips at other students, tear his assignments into tiny pieces and bully younger kids on the playground.

Nobody was surprised when he signed up for band in fifth grade. His other teachers assumed he was looking for an excuse to leave class for 30 minutes twice a week and add my name to the list of adults he enjoyed terrorizing. I was taken aback by the fact that he wanted to play the trumpet. (I had him pegged as a drummer for sure!)

The first few weeks of band were exactly as I expected. Brandon never paid attention, never had his music, and quickly secured a chair right at the front of the classroom where I could keep my eye on him. I tried everything with this student. I met with his parents and his classroom teacher. I had behavior plans and incentive charts. Nothing worked and my time and energy were quickly draining. At the end of the first semester, after I started to receive complaints from other parents that Brandon was inhibiting their child's ability to participate, I had to have a heart-to-heart with Brandon's mom about dropping her son from band.

After a lengthy conversation, we agreed to give him one last chance. This was against my better judgment, but I just couldn't say no to this parent who was obviously also at her wits' end.

A few weeks into the new semester, Brandon actually had a semi-good day. He came into class without causing a disruption, got out his trumpet, played along the whole time, and even volunteered to answer a question. I was shocked! I praised him over and over for his improved behavior, but he seemed unfazed.

As I wrapped up my work at the end of the day, I wondered if the day's experience had been a fluke. I considered calling Brandon's mom to tell her about the positive change I witnessed, but when I saw the lengthy to-do list on my desk, I realized I didn't have time for another half-hour talk with her. I left school without giving it another thought.

When I got home that night, after stepping away from the situation for a bit, I realized I was being ridiculous. I had all of my band parents' emails in my address book. It would take less than a minute to drop Brandon's mom a quick email telling her about his progress. I signed into my account from home and pecked out a few sentences.

Dear Sheila,

I wanted to let you know that I saw a complete 180-degree shift in Brandon's behavior in band today. I knew there was a motivated student in there somewhere and he definitely let that side of him show today. Thank you for working with him. If this behavior continues, I am confident he will find great success with band in the future.

There. Done. Less than 100 words and 1 minute of my time.

When I got to school the next morning, I was greeted with a tearful voicemail from Brandon's mom.

Mrs. Schwartz, you have no idea how much your email made an impact on my son and our family. I am so afraid to read letters from the school because they are always bad. I have never had a teacher take the time to tell me that my son actually did something good or would ever be successful in anything. When I shared your email with Brandon, he flashed a smile from ear to ear. Thank you. As a mother, that is the best thing I can ever hope for.

She also left the same message for my principal who promptly called me into her office and thanked me for making such a positive impact at the school.

That day marked the end of my problems with Brandon. From that point on, he was the model band student. I could not have been happier. Sure, he still had his moments of inattention or defiance, but nothing more than I would expect from any 10-year-old.

That short email — the one that took *less than 1 minute of my time* and I almost decided I was "too busy" to send — ended up providing one of the best teaching moments of the year.

Don't Forget Your Grace Notes

Any master musician will tell you that it's the small details that separate a mediocre performance from a great one. Every single note is important; even the tiny grace notes and the quick ornamentations. Glossing over those small details in your preparation can cause the whole performance to suffer.

We need to think the same way when we consider time management. It's often the smallest tasks that make the biggest difference.

Strategy: If it Takes Less Than 5 Minutes, Do it Now!

Short little tasks that only take a few minutes of our time are the easiest to put off. We say we'll "do them later" because they don't seem important right now. The problem is that these tiny tasks are the Vegetables in our Time Diet and as any 7-year-old can tell you, swirling the vegetables around your plate will not make them disappear.

If a task is placed in front of you and you know it will take less than 5 minutes to finish, do it right away, or at the very least, do it before you leave at the end of the day. These little Vegetable tasks seem insignificant at first, but if you put them off and forget about them, they have a way of blowing up into enormous Meat tasks that are going to take a big chunk of time to complete.

Paperwork

One of the worst offenders of the 5-Minute Rule is paperwork. It seems that every task a teacher does during the day comes with a myriad of forms to fill out first. I have yet to meet the teacher who actually enjoys filling out all these papers, but it is a necessary part of the job.

We all know what it's like to be passing by the office and see a bright neon form sitting in our mailbox. Our gut reaction might be to pretend we didn't see it and just keep walking, but we know we can't just let it sit there. Reluctantly, we grab it from our box with an Academy-Award-worthy "sigh" and pretend to read it. Then we'll mumble something incoherently to ourselves about why the district wastes paper printing all these forms when they could use that money to pay teacher salaries.

Finally, we add the form to one of the many piles on our desk and forget about it. We promise ourselves that we'll fill it out "later," but "later" never happens.

The truth about paperwork is that you'll never feel any *more* inclined to fill it out than when it first touches your hand.

When you put it off and it ends up in the black hole of papers on your desk, the school secretary will have to chase you down after the deadline has passed. This makes more work for everyone involved. Chances are, you'll need to find that paper again at the least convenient time, and suddenly that tiny little form becomes a big problem. Remember, your secretary probably couldn't care less about the form either, but it's his or her *job* to care.

We can't afford to upset our secretaries. Not only is it extremely unprofessional to deliberately make more work for someone else, but it doesn't do us any favors either. Our secretaries are the ones who give us extra keys when we forget ours, let us have more copy paper when our stash is gone, and can make getting a Purchase Order either a smooth process or a nightmare.

The next time you catch yourself putting off a tiny Vegetable piece of paperwork, stop. Just do it and be done with it. You'll save yourself time in the long run.

Other Short Tasks

Paperwork isn't the only short little Vegetable task we put off on a regular basis. Here are a few other common tasks we put off that cost us more time later:

1. Parent communication

Remember, staying in touch with parents doesn't have to take a lot of time. A quick note or email takes only a moment. You don't have to risk getting drawn into a lengthy conversation, and the communication can pay enormous dividends later.

2. Follow-up calls

Always take the time to check in frequently with any vendor you're working with, whether it is the travel agent planning your annual tour or the fundraising company coordinating your upcoming cookie dough sale. A quick check to make sure they have everything they need from you may save tons of time and headache later.

3. Helping colleagues

It's never a good idea to put everyone else's needs before your own, but it's all too easy to put your peers *last* and that isn't fair. If a colleague needs a small piece of information, or an answer to a quick question, you should make every effort to respond by the end of the day. Waiting for your 30-second answer may be holding up hours of work for them. Think of it as "Time Management Karma." Treat others' time the way you'd want your time to be treated.

Review

Sometimes the tasks that cause us the most trouble are the ones that require the least time to complete.

1. Quick tasks, like parent communication, make more of a difference than you realize.

2. Adhere to the 5-Minute Rule. If it takes less than 5 minutes, do it now, not later.

3. Don't put off your paperwork. It won't go away and will not become any more pleasant or convenient later!

Remember, these tiny little tasks are the "grace notes" of your teaching. The mediocre players won't give them much thought, but the truly great performers know that every detail needs attention.

4

PUT A FERMATA ON YOUR PREP TIME

"Mrs. Schwartz, what's this thing on top of the last note of our song?"

While I was disappointed that Nikki hadn't grasped the concept of a fermata the first three times I'd explained it, I didn't want to discourage her from asking questions, so I explained it again.

"That's called a fermata, remember? It means to hold the note longer than its full value. That's why I asked you to circle it, so you'll remember to look up at me and watch for the cutoff."

Nikki stared quizzically at the new symbol she had just learned, her clarinet inching closer and closer to rolling off of her lap.

"But...it's a whole note. Doesn't it just get four beats?" she asked.

"Right, Nikki. Normally it would, but because it has a fermata on top we're going to hold it out longer."

Nikki nodded slowly as she continued to stare at her music.

"But...that just doesn't make any sense, Mrs. Schwartz. I mean, you could just hold it out...forever!"

"Yes Nikki, I suppose I could."

That was the end of the fermata discussion. The next time I saw Nikki's band class, I noticed that she was writing something on the board as I was trying to pull a stuck mouthpiece from her classmate's trumpet.

Nikki had modified my lesson plan on the board. I had written the order of the pieces I planned to rehearse that day, and she had drawn a big fermata on top of the first piece, "Dragon Slayer."

I chuckled a little bit at her creative application of the symbol she'd learned.

"What's this, Nikki?" I asked.

"Well, Mrs. Schwartz, Dragon Slayer is an awesome piece and the rest of them are pretty lame so I want to make Dragon Slayer last as long as possible."

I smiled as I turned and erased the other pieces from the board. "OK Nikki, just for you, we will focus on Dragon Slayer today."

Strategy: Maximize Your Prep Time

Wouldn't it be cool if we could simply put fermatas on everything that we wish would last a little longer? In real life, we can't exactly do that, but that doesn't mean we can't do everything possible to utilize each and every available minute. Prep time can be scarce in teaching jobs — especially music teaching jobs — since we so often have students clamoring to get into our rooms. Those few golden minutes of blissful productivity seem to melt away before they've even started.

There is a difference between simply *filling* your prep time and *maximizing* it. Filling time just means that you are busy doing something. Maximizing it means you are efficiently squeezing every last drop of productivity out of each minute. This means you have a far greater chance of being able to leave work at a decent time in the afternoon without bringing heaps of schoolwork home with you.

Analyze Your Energy

One of the easiest ways to start getting your work done more efficiently is to analyze when you have the most energy and when you have the least. Then schedule your work accordingly. For example, I am a morning person. When I get to work in the morning, I am fully energized the moment I sit down at my desk...then it's all downhill from there.

Knowing this, I get to work a little early so I can get a few good Meat tasks done while my energy is high before the students arrive. Then, when the students leave at the end of the day, I do my Vegetable tasks because I don't have the energy to do anything remotely difficult. If I tried to do my complex Meat tasks at the end of the day, I'd be wasting my time. I'd be so exhausted that my work would take three times longer than it should.

Maybe you don't work like this. Maybe you are like some of my colleagues who are hardly awake when they stumble into school in the morning and need a few cups of coffee to get going before the students arrive. If that's true, then you'll want to reverse your workload and do the easier things in the morning and the more difficult things in the afternoon when your energy has kicked in. Sometimes an easy switch like that can save hours of time during the teaching week.

Get Rid of Time Killers

Another great way to stay focused during your prep time and get as much done as possible is to get rid of your Time Killers.

Time Killers are those little things that waste our time without our permission. You might more easily recognize the Time Killers that plague you at home, such as the internet, television, email, phone calls, snacking, etc...Surely you've experienced a day in which you're at home trying to work and then BAM! All of a sudden you're in the kitchen eating a snack, or at your computer scrolling through Facebook. You don't know how it happened. It's as though your mouse-clicking fingers had a mind of their own.

Time Killers aren't necessarily bad by themselves. However, they *become* bad when they distract you from your work. As soon as you're distracted, it takes time to regain your focus and your work starts to take longer. This is why you must eliminate your Time Killers *before* they have a chance to distract you. This could mean working in a different place, closing your internet browser, or coming up with other solutions to eliminate the temptations.

The Time Killers I've outlined above aren't necessarily a problem in our teaching lives. After all, our districts do a pretty good job of removing these types of things for us! However, we do have *different* types of Time Killers that we face every day at work.

Do Not Disturb

As music teachers, our students can sometimes interrupt our productivity during non-class time. As we all know, the music room is *the* cool place to be on campus. During break, at lunch, after school, before school — students are always clamoring to get into the music room. Often they are there to practice, but sometimes they are just there because they love you and they love music and they want to spend every moment possible in your room.

We want our students to feel this way about the music room, but we also need time to prepare lessons and materials for them. We can't work very efficiently when students are drawing on the whiteboard or playing hide-and-seek in the instrument cubbies.

You can still encourage students to come in to the music room to practice and ask questions, but it's important to set boundaries as to when that can and can't happen.

At least once a week, I set aside a time when a "Do Not Disturb" sign hangs on the door. This allows me some uninterrupted time to get a good start on my to-do list before the students come rushing in for class.

Delegate to Students

When you *do* decide to let students into your room, don't be afraid to put them to work! The type of student who wants to hang out in the music room all the time is usually the same type of student who would love nothing more than a chance to help his or her favorite teacher.

Think of some small Vegetable tasks you can delegate to these eager students. It will keep them occupied and will also take a few things off of your plate. While it might initially take a little longer to train students how to do these tasks, it will save you time in the long run.

Suggestions for Student Delegated Tasks

1. Daily room set-up and clean-up

2. Music library organization

3. Helping younger students

4. Alphabetizing

5. Running errands to the office

Is What You're Doing Worth It?

Finally, as you're trying to complete your to-do list as efficiently as possible, it's important to consider whether the things on your list are actually worth the time you're spending on them. Sometimes it's difficult for music teachers to answer this question honestly because it's hard to admit that we've been doing something that's not necessary. However, it's important to keep evaluating and making sure our time is being used in the best way possible.

The Case of the Practice Records

Ever since I joined band in sixth grade, I filled out a practice record every week. Some teachers had us write in the back of our method books. Others had their own forms for us to fill out. Either way, for the better part of seven years, I diligently logged my weekly practice time for my parents to sign.

Then, when I began my student teaching, my mentor teacher also required his students to fill out practice records. I dutifully sat in the back of the classroom and graded them each week as I became rather well-versed in detecting a 13-year-old's attempt to copy Mom's signature.

Naturally, when I started my first teaching job, I required my students to fill out practice records because at this point in my music experience, I thought that's just what you're supposed to do.

Each week for the first few months of school, I collected them, graded them, recorded them, and passed them back to all eighty-five students. It was a bit of a pain, but that's what I thought all good band directors did.

However, my students weren't practicing.

What had worked for nearly every other music teacher in my life wasn't working for me. I was wasting my time.

I rethought the entire process. I talked to other teachers in my district to find out what I was doing wrong, and was surprised to find out that many of them didn't even do practice records at all! After a little trial and error, I came up with a different system. Since many of these students lived in apartment complexes and couldn't practice at home, I held sectionals before school or at recess for them to practice in small groups. I put a rating scale of 1-10 up on the board for each one of our pieces and the students could collectively decide when the band sounded good enough to move up to the next number. When the piece was concert-ready it received the honor of being labeled a "10." I ove this!

My students now had an incentive to work hard and the means to practice outside of class. This is what the practice records had set out to achieve, but now we were accomplishing those same goals in a new way. (And I didn't have to spend my valuable time grading sheets of paper that ultimately didn't mean anything.)

Re-Think Your To-Do List

The point of that story is not to say practice records are a waste of time. They are a great tool for many teachers, but they weren't working in my particular teaching situation. We can't waste our time doing things that aren't working simply because they work for others. Here are a few strategies to help you re-think your to-do list:

1. Seek out professional development opportunities such as state music education conferences to look for new ideas.

2. Ask other music teachers in your district how they do things, and if those things have worked.

3. Talk to teachers in other subject areas. Some of my best organizational ideas have come from kindergarten teachers.

4. When in doubt, ask the students! They have better ideas than you might give them credit for and are pretty candid about telling you what is and isn't working.

The Myth of Staying Late

Prep time is a precious commodity when you're a music teacher. Maximize it in order to limit your chances of taking work home or staying late at school on a regular basis.

Be careful not to fall into the trap of striving to be the school martyr. I've heard music teachers boast to their colleagues that they are always the first car in the parking lot and the last one out. Working hard is important, but just because your work takes longer doesn't mean you're doing a better job. The old saying about quality vs. quantity is key.

While it's important to make sure your face is seen frequently around campus, your entry and exit time to the parking lot is not the measure of your worth as a teacher. What you actually accomplish is.

Review

While we can't make prep time last forever, we can maximize it and make it seem longer than before.

1. Analyze your energy. Try to avoid doing your most difficult tasks when you are the most exhausted. This makes work take longer.

2. Set aside a student-free time during the week to get things done without distractions.

3. Delegate. Students love to help you. Let them.

4. Make sure your tasks are worth it. Constantly re-evaluate your teaching practices to make sure you are making the most efficient use of your time.

Maximizing your prep time rather than simply "filling" it is a way to put a fermata over those precious minutes and make them seem longer. Just don't forget to watch for the cutoff.

Emily Schwartz

5

NEVER REHEARSE WITHOUT A SCORE

Everyone has probably had a student like my little trumpet player Andrew. This boy lived and breathed for band class. He was a decent player, but a bit of a "know-it-all." He loved to "accidentally" keep playing after the cutoff so everyone could hear how well he knew his part. It was not uncommon for him to call out his classmates for not articulating correctly or for missing an accidental.

One morning, while Andrew was in the band room clamoring for my attention, he declared, "You know Mrs. Schwartz, I have been practicing so hard that now I have all of my music memorized."

"That's great Andrew," I said, with the best teacher-enthusiasm I could muster. I was proud of him for how hard he worked, but his constant "look what I can do!" attitude was wearing thin, especially since I knew he would jump at the first chance to rub it in his classmates' faces.

During band that day, Andrew's eyes where everywhere except on the music stand in front of him. He was looking up at the ceiling, down at the carpet, over at the clock...basically doing everything he could to prove to me that he was *not* looking at his music. (Because, of course, he had it memorized!)

Unwilling to give in to his desperate plea for attention, I let this go on several days longer than I probably should have.

Apparently, Andrew was unconvinced that everyone in the room had noticed his memorization skills, so one day, instead of sitting in his usual spot in the middle of the trumpet section, he pulled up a chair several feet away from the rest of the band. He very purposefully did not put a music stand in front of him, and began to get out his things.

One could only marvel at his determination!

"Andrew, please grab your stand and sit with the other trumpet players," I said as I walked over to his corner of the room.

"Mrs. Schwartz, I don't *need* music. I have it memorized!" he announced very loudly to the band.

"I'm proud of you Andrew," I said calmly, "but I would really appreciate it if you got your music out and sat in your spot."

"Ugh! That is *so* unfair," he scoffed. "What is the point of having music if I have it all in my head!"

"Well, Andrew," I began, "this is not the first time I've played the piece 'Anasazi' with a band before. In fact, I've done it several different years now with several different groups of students. Would you say there is a fair chance that I have it memorized?"

He nodded.

"You're right," I continued. "If you were to name any measure number right now and any instrument in the band, I would more than likely be able to tell you what notes that instrument should be playing. However, what do you see up on my music stand?"

Andrew said nothing.

"Music!" the entire flute section cried.

"Right, because even though I know the parts really well, I still like to have a score out while we are rehearsing so that I have a reminder. I *could* use my brain power to remember everybody's part, but I'd much rather put it to work helping you all get better. I can quickly look down at my score to shout out measure numbers, dynamics and other details that I might forget otherwise.

So Andrew, I *appreciate* that you have it memorized but I'd really like you to have your music in front of you as a backup."

"Fine..." he mumbled with an eye roll that would make any teenager proud.

We proceeded with the rehearsal. Andrew put his music back on his stand, but continued to make an obvious point of not looking at it. That's fine. I had made my point.

However, toward the end of class I stopped the band to work on the trumpet melody at measure 19. (Beginning band directors everywhere are smiling right now because they know exactly which B-natural the trumpets were missing.)

"Trumpets, can I hear you play that part at 19?"

I watched Andrew. I saw him freeze. I saw the wheels turning in his head. He didn't remember where that was but was too proud to look at his music.

Right before the downbeat, I saw him glance quickly down at his stand. It was only for a moment, but the look on his face told me that he knew I saw him.

None of his other classmates saw this happen and I resisted the temptation to point it out.

It would be our little secret.

Strategy: Keep A Calendar

We can all chuckle at Andrew's story because we understand students' need to impress us. However, I've seen adults give the same kinds of excuses for not writing their obligations down in a calendar.

"I've tried to use calendars before, but I never look at them because I just know what I'm supposed to do."

"I don't really need to write things down, I can remember them all."

We're all smart, college-educated people. We can *all* do a pretty good job of remembering most things...until we *don't* and we miss a deadline. This is why it's essential to write down all of your obligations in an organized way.

To be clear, this does not mean you have to have a pristine, neat, color-coded calendar. This simply means you have to have a system that works for *you*.

Two Components of a Time Management System

Fortunately, it only takes two things to have a good, organized system of time management in your teaching job:

1. A calendar for long-term deadlines

2. A list for daily tasks

These two things can take a variety of different forms depending on your needs and preferences. As long as you have them both, it doesn't matter what they look like as long as you use them consistently.

The Calendar

The purpose of the calendar is to give you a broad picture of your upcoming responsibilities. When asked, many teachers say they keep some sort of calendar, but often this only includes things like school holidays, parent conferences and staff meetings. If you aren't putting *every* deadline, even the small ones, in your calendar, then you're less likely to look at it frequently. A calendar that you only look at occasionally becomes merely a reference material, not a productivity tool.

Think of your calendar like a giant "data dump" for your brain. This is where you put every deadline, every appointment, and every event. Even if you're pretty sure you'll remember it, write it down. Usually, it's the deadlines we were "sure" we'd remember that we end up missing the most frequently.

Using Start Dates and Due Dates

As you're writing things down in your calendar, it's important to put in *more* than just deadlines. Deadlines and due dates are great, but they only tell you one piece of information: when the task needs to be finished.

For every due date you write down in your calendar you should also write a corresponding *start date.* A due date is just the finish line. A start date tells you when to start working on a task.

For example, let's say you are taking your orchestra to a festival in March. The deadline to send in registration is January 18. If you simply write "Festival Registration Due" in your calendar on January 18th, you are very likely to wait until that day to send it in. You now run the risk of not having the right form, payment, or signature and may have to send it in a day late.

However, if you also assign a start date to this due date, you are far more likely to think about it earlier. You can write "Fill Out Festival Registration" on January 10th. Now you've just made a plan that you will start the registration process early and when January 10th arrives, you'll be far more likely to do it because you've written it down. When we procrastinate, it isn't necessarily because we are lazy or too busy, it's because we either forget or haven't promised ourselves a specific day we'll begin. Start dates solve that problem.

Due dates are set by *other people*. Start dates are set by *you*. By using start dates in your calendar, you put yourself in a position of control. You will not only organize your obligations so you won't forget about them, but more importantly, you'll organize and plan your time so you can complete everything more efficiently.

The List

The second component of a good time management system is a list for daily tasks. As music teachers, we are pulled in a million different directions. Sometimes it can be difficult to stay focused. While having a calendar is important for keeping track of your "big picture" schedule, your daily list is where you keep a running record of everything you need to accomplish in a given day. This is where you jot things down such as "return parent phone call," "finish drill design," "copy information letters," or "order music."

When you get that brief moment of prep time, just consult the list and start crossing things off. With a daily list, you don't have to waste any time or focus trying to remember what to do. Every moment you waste between tasks increases the likelihood that you'll get distracted, get off track, and stop working efficiently.

Maintaining a list also stops you from jumping haphazardly from one task to the next. We're teachers. Our brains move a

44

mile a minute. (We have to or we'd never be able to stay one step ahead of our students!) However, when we sit down to work, this slightly spastic mental state can work against us. Choose one thing on the list, finish it, and cross it off. Then move on to the next thing.

As with the calendar, it's important to write *everything* down on your list. Remember to include not only your Meats, but also your Vegetables and Desserts. Too often we write only the big things down on our lists. This causes us to procrastinate on the smaller Vegetable tasks until they become immediate problems. Use the start dates on your calendar as a guide for making your list each day. Then add any meetings, rehearsals, or events you need to attend as well as miscellaneous tasks. Not only does this help keep you focused and organized, but getting everything down on paper makes you feel less stressed.

What Type of List and Calendar?

Your calendar and list can take many different forms as long as they:

1. Are easy to use

2. Are transportable

3. Work for you

I hesitate to recommend one specific type of calendar or list because I only know what type works for *me.* It might not be the same type that works for you.

I prefer to keep a paper list and calendar. My list is simply a small pad of paper with a pen attached and my calendar is a monthly pocket calendar that's less than half an inch thick. I keep both in my teacher bag and carry them everywhere I go. Since I travel between three different schools during the day, I need something that is very portable. I also prefer to keep a paper list and calendar because I enjoy the flexibility they offer. I can star things, circle things, and draw arrows to items easily with just the stroke of a pen. While I use technology for many other parts of my life, I prefer to keep track of my time management on paper.

If you prefer to use technology, just make sure it is easy. There are hundreds of calendar applications for your phone or laptop. Just because one of them is popular doesn't necessarily mean it will work for you. When selecting your digital calendar, consider the following things:

1. Ease of data entry

If it takes more than one or two clicks to enter information into your calendar, you won't do it on a consistent basis.

2. Sync capabilities

If you want to keep track of your time on your computer, consider choosing an application that also syncs to your phone so you have access to your information while away from your desk or classroom. You want to be able to add things to your calendar as soon as you find out about them. If you have to wait until you get back to your computer, you're more likely to forget. Besides, some music teachers are only at their computers for a brief time during the school day.

3. Personal preference

If a particular application isn't working for you, don't waste your time trying to make it work. Try something different. Frequently, when people think they have poor time management skills it's really just because they are trying to force themselves to use a system that doesn't work for them. Try either a different application or a paper calendar.

Ditch the Excuses

Finally, if you're serious about using your time more efficiently and finally getting out in front of your deadlines, you must commit to stop making excuses. We are well-versed in the excuses students use to get out of things:

"I didn't have time to practice."

"My instrument is in the shop."

or, my personal favorite,

"It's the reed."

Music teachers have their own set of excuses for not keeping themselves organized:

"I don't like to write things down."

"I'm too busy to keep track of everything."

"I went to music school. All we did was practice. Why would I have needed time management skills?"

These are all hurdles, but they are not impossible to overcome. Your stress level will thank you. (And so will your students. They don't like you when you're stressed and grumpy.)

Review

Just like you would never rehearse without a score, you should never try to manage your time without a written system.

1. Keep a list and a calendar. Be sure to write down all deadlines and reference them frequently.

2. Use start dates. Every due date in your calendar should have a corresponding start date. This way you are making a written promise to yourself to begin your work.

3. Use what works for you. If you don't like the kind of calendar you're using, change it. Just because something works for others doesn't mean it will work for you.

The most important part of having a time management system is to consistency. If you have the discipline to make it a habit, you'll see amazing gains in your productivity.

6

DON'T BE TACET AT STAFF MEETINGS

I wish I had a picture of my face during my first staff meeting. It was something between the confused look students give us the first time we teach them 6/8 time and the sigh of frustration you experience when you realize you're about to be stuck in traffic for an hour.

Cleverly-constructed acronyms were being tossed around like grains of rice at a wedding. Excel spreadsheets with rows and rows of percentages and test scores were shown on a severely outdated version of PowerPoint. Sometimes these charts made people clap, so I clapped too. Sometimes they elicited sighs and grumbling comments that began with, "See, this is the problem with education..." I nodded in agreement.

I had come dutifully prepared with a notepad and pen to write down pertinent updates. I waited with my pen hovering over the first line, ready to record all of the information that would help me teach my students — the information that would help me get a better understanding of how to deal with the challenges of my new classroom.

I left the meeting with a sense of bewilderment...and a blank piece of paper.

"None of this applies to me," I thought. "I don't even understand half the things they are saying. It's like they are speaking a different language. I need help learning how to use the copier and teaching my sixth graders how to play in E-flat. When are we going to talk about that?"

As the semester progressed, I found many ways to keep myself from falling asleep during these bi-weekly meetings. Sometimes I counted ceiling tiles. Other times I kept a tally of how many times different buzzwords were tossed around. ("Bloom's Taxonomy" once received a whopping score of 23.)

Later that year, I lamented these encounters to a more senior band director in the district, expecting to get a little sympathy and bond over a shared experience. "Why in the world do they make us go to these things?" I asked.

"Well," he said, "I'm actually very grateful for staff meetings." He let that statement linger for a few moments before he continued. "Music teachers love to complain that nobody at their school understands what they do. I figure, I can't complain about that unless I've made an honest attempt to understand what *everyone else* at my school does. Staff meetings are a great opportunity for that."

I sat there dumbfounded. I had been so busy telling myself that nothing applied to me, that I hadn't bothered to look for any other meaning or usefulness in these mandatory meetings.

My attitude began to change. I started to listen more closely to what was going on and asked questions if I didn't understand something. I learned how reading blocks and interventions are set up. I learned how students are classified according to test scores. I started deciphering all of the education acronyms and understanding what they meant. Pretty soon I found myself using "education jargon" in conversations with other staff members in the copy room.

I was learning the "language" of the school, and that made me feel more a part of it.

One afternoon at a staff meeting, the principal announced that all teachers needed to add 30 minutes to their reading block for intervention time. Since I now understood what all of that meant, I could sympathize with the riot that ensued.

"They don't have those extra 30 minutes in their schedules," I thought to myself. "They can't do that. There just aren't enough minutes in the school day."

A few weeks later, I found myself in a similar battle against time. I needed to schedule an extra rehearsal with my band students before the concert. Between assemblies, testing, and school holidays we had missed several rehearsals and our music was just not concert-ready.

I was running out of time and since the majority of my school population relied on the school bus for transportation, an after-school rehearsal was not an option. No, I would have to find a way to convince the classroom teachers to let me have their students outside the regularly scheduled band time.

I ran into one of the fifth grade teachers in the copy room later that week.

"Tanya," I began, "I can't believe they are throwing that additional reading block time at you. Like you weren't crunched enough for time already, right? How are you handling it?"

"Oh my goodness, it's horrible," she replied. "I have so many great science lessons prepared, but we haven't gotten to them all week. By the time we get through reading and math, there just isn't enough time."

"I know what you mean," I said. "We haven't had time to do our final run-through for the concert. I'm afraid the kids just won't be ready."

I took a deep breath and prepared to ask for her help.

"Hey, do you think we can help each other out? If I can take your kids for an extra hour next week for a rehearsal, then after the concert is finished, I can let them out a little early so you can have some more time for science."

"Absolutely Emily! I don't know how you get all those wild animals to sit still and play music."

Not only did I get my extra rehearsal, but the next day I found a note in my mailbox.

Dear Emily,

Thank you for being so understanding of the time crunch we're all facing. I often get frustrated at specialists who demand to see the students all the time and seem to have little regard for all of the things I need to accomplish as well. Your professionalism speaks very highly of your program. Any time you need a little extra help before concert time just let me know. I will make it happen.

Sincerely,

Tanya

Strategy: Don't Let Meetings Waste Your Time

I made a pivotal mistake my first year of teaching. I wasted so much energy complaining about meetings and never once tried to find a way to make them worthwhile. Meetings were only wasting my time because I was allowing them to do so.

Change Your Attitude

Attending meetings is a necessary part of the job description, but they are a notoriously dreaded activity. Some might even consider them to be the "Brussels sprouts" of tasks in their Time Diet — the least desirable Vegetable.

Since you can't change the fact that meetings are mandatory, the only thing you *can* change is your attitude. If you go into them thinking, "This is going to be a huge waste of my time," and continue to think about all the other things you could be doing instead, then you're right; nothing productive will come from you being there for an hour.

However, if you go into a meeting thinking, "What can I gain from this?" and, "How can I use this meeting to help my teaching and strengthen my relationship with my school and my colleagues?" then you will find yourself gaining more from that hour-long meeting than you thought.

Make Your Own Connections

A good portion of staff meetings often includes some sort of professional development. This is usually when the music and P.E teachers start to zone out because the teaching techniques rarely seem relevant to these "special" subject areas.

Just because the connections to your discipline aren't made explicitly clear, that doesn't mean you can't gain anything from the information. You simply have to make those connections yourself.

Advocate

Staff meetings are also a great opportunity to advocate for your program. Music teachers love to get together and say that nobody appreciates how hard they work. Well, have you *told* anyone recently?

As the principal is going through upcoming events, make sure your concerts are mentioned. Tell everyone to get excited about the theme for next year's field show. Point out that an orchestra student just entered a composition contest. Make sure everyone knows about the good you do at the school and for your students. Yes, it's bragging a bit, but that's part of what advocacy is all about.

Meet Other People

Being a music teacher can be isolating. While the English department may have five or six other teachers, the music department might be just...you. Even if you aren't by yourself, you probably have at most one or two other people and even they might travel between two or three schools.

If you've ever caught yourself saying, "I'm just so busy. I don't have time to really meet anyone else at the school," utilize the staff meeting! It may be the only time you'll have a chance to meet the teachers that work on the other side of the building.

If you're new to the school, or you've just always kept to yourself, make it a point to converse with one "new" person at each meeting. Not only will the extra effort bring you closer to your colleagues, but it can also open doors to learning from teachers in other disciplines. I have picked up some of my best teaching tips from kindergarten teachers, school counselors, and coaches.

When You're In Charge

Often, our time is at the mercy of the principal or other administrator who is running the meeting. However, sometimes that person may be you. In this case, it's important to practice good "meeting karma:" stay organized, keep on topic, and move quickly.

If you are asked to give a presentation at a staff meeting, resist the temptation to be long-winded. (I know, I know, we're music teachers. It's what we do. You'll have to restrain yourself.) Jot down a few points you need to make and be brief. People are far more likely to listen to what you have to say if they know you value their time.

If you're meeting as a department, or as a small group of teachers, never begin the meeting without an agenda. A meeting without an agenda is like a road trip without a map — you might end up getting somewhere, but it's going to take a really long time.

With input from the group, collect a list of things to talk about before the meeting starts. Make sure everyone has a copy of the list and stays on topic. Meetings can quickly morph into gripe or chit-chat sessions. This kind of social interaction can be important, but is best saved for after the meeting!

When you end the meeting, whether it is a curriculum planning session, a department meeting, or a school committee, make sure all participants leave knowing what they need to accomplish.

I was once on the Talent Show Committee for my school. The first time we got together, everyone was bursting with ideas. We were going to streamline the after-school audition process to make it easier on parents. We agreed on a timeline for when forms would go home, what the rejection letters would say, and who would emcee the whole thing.

As we wound down the meeting, I felt pretty good about what we'd accomplished, but as I was about to walk out the door I realized, "I have no idea what I'm supposed to do next with this project."

We hadn't decided who was going to write the letters, copy the papers, put the announcement in the bulletin, or anything like that. We had a lot of good ideas, but if we ended this meeting without a plan, it would be as if that hour never happened. What a waste of our time. Then we'd have to schedule *another* meeting later to talk about all the things that hadn't been decided.

We sat back down for another few minutes and determined who was going to do what. Now everyone knew his or her specific action items. Those few extra minutes saved us hours down the line. We didn't have to meet again as a committee until just before the auditions.

Don't leave a meeting until you know if you have an action item to complete. It will save everyone loads of time down the road.

Review

Meetings are a necessary part of any teaching job. The way in which you approach them will determine whether they are useful resources or wastes of your time.

1. Learn the language. Use staff meetings as a way to learn more about the school and the challenges other teachers face. Make your own connections from the meeting agenda to the music curriculum.

2. Advocate. Music programs only survive if people value them. Use staff meetings as a chance to let everyone know what your program does.

3. Practice good "meeting karma." When you are in charge of a meeting, make sure it runs efficiently.

Your staff meeting agenda doesn't have the word "Tacet" on it. Change your attitude to make meetings worthwhile.

7

STRESS LEVEL: SEMPRE MEZZO FORTE

Close your eyes and think of every stereotype you've ever known about trombone players. Matt was all of those things. And more.

During recruiting day, I had Matt pegged as the class clown after the first few seconds I met him. He was a rowdy kid. Not in a malicious, "I'm trying to make trouble" kind of way, but rather, "I'm desperate for everyone's attention and will do anything to get it."

When the time came to sign up for instruments, he asked, "Which one is the loudest?"

"The clarinet," I told him.

He saw right through my feeble attempt to save my ears from what would surely be a daily struggle when he found his calling as either a brass or percussion player.

"I want to play THAT," he exclaimed pointing to the trombone sitting on my desk.

"OK," I thought to myself. "At least it isn't drums. Maybe I can work with this."

As it turns out, Matt was a pretty good trombone player. He caught on quickly and ended up being one of the strongest players in band that year. The problem was that Matt's volume level was stuck on *fortissimo*. Constantly.

Loud doesn't even begin to describe it. Matt's sound was like a dagger that cut right through the rest of the band. Every note he played was correct, but it was the most piercing, overblown sound you'd ever heard. I pulled out every strategy I knew to get him to play softer, but nothing worked.

During one of my frequent after-class meetings with Matt, I finally reached the end of my rope.

"Matt," I sighed. "I don't know what else to do. I might have to switch you to another instrument."

"You don't understand Mrs. Schwartz!" he exclaimed, as he usually did. "I *can't* play softer. I just can't."

"Yes you can!" I said in exasperation. "Matt, you're a talented musician. I know you can do this. You just have to find some control over your sound."

He looked down at the floor for a few moments. "Mrs. Schwartz, I think I can probably do it but...well...it's just *easier* to play loud."

That was the first time he'd ever admitted that to me.

"You're right Matt. It *is* easier to be out-of-control. But really great musicians learn to control their sound and I *know* you can be a really great musician."

Matt started meeting with me before school for lessons. Gradually, he got his tone under control and started learning how to blend into the ensemble.

I even made him his own "dynamics chart" similar to the one I had posted on the wall for the rest of the students. However, while the wall chart went up to *fortissimo*, Matt's only went up to *mezzo forte*.

Matt would always continue to err on the side of "loud" on the dynamics continuum, but he had drastically improved his ability to control his tone and sound.

One day I overheard one of his trumpet friends bragging that his trumpet was now louder than Matt's trombone.

"Psh, whatever," he laughed. "I can play soft and that's harder."

9:36am: A trombone player bragged about playing softly.

That was a statement for the record books.

Strategy: Don't Let Stressing Out Waste Your Time

Teachers who graduated from college with a music degree, have surely mastered the control of dynamics on their instrument. However, if we were to express our stress level in terms of musical dynamics, we might admit that it's hard to keep it below a steady *fortissimo* at certain points of the year.

Not only is a high stress level unhealthy, it can cause our work to take much longer. Some degree of stress is a natural part of life, but when it becomes a regular state of mind, stress can be extremely detrimental. We feel tired all the time. We start feeling overwhelmed and convincing ourselves that we simply can't get everything done. These kinds of feelings are the fat in your Time Diet that must be removed.

Remember, playing the trombone too loudly is easy. Allowing yourself to always feel stressed is easy too. Controlling stress is difficult, but it can be done. With practice and patience, you too can keep your stress level at a steady *mezzo forte*.

Delegate

"If you want something done right, you have to do it yourself." That phrase is responsible for a great deal of unnecessary stress in music teachers' jobs. You *can't* do everything yourself and you shouldn't even try. Parents, students, booster organizations, other teachers, and community members are all eager to help you if you let them.

If you have difficulty letting go of tasks, ask yourself if you are truly worried the task won't be done *right* or if it just won't be done *your way.* If it's the latter, learn to accept that there are many of ways of doing things and that your decreased stress level is worth letting other people do things *their* way.

However, if you've tried delegating in the past and the task truly hasn't been correctly, try these steps of effective delegation:

1. Give clear expectations

Especially when delegating to parents and students, make sure you have given clear directions and expectations as to the completion of the task. It's extra helpful to make sure these expectations are in writing. For example, if you are asking your booster president to order buses, make sure your instructions also include following up with the bus company the day before your trip to confirm the order.

2. Make time for training

If you're able to delegate the same kinds of tasks to the same people frequently, you increase their chances of success. If you take the time to train your student leadership council to set the stage for your concert, they'll be able to do it for the rest of the year.

3. Avoid "return to sender" tasks

If you put parents in charge of a fundraiser, yet they email you every day asking you to do things for them, then you haven't actually delegated the task. Empower your "employees" to complete the task all the way through and do not allow the task to be given back to you.

The biggest thing to remember when delegating is that you shouldn't just delegate the tiniest Vegetable tasks of your Time Diet. It's easy to ask a student to put one little paper away, or to ask a parent to make one phone call for you. It's tougher to let someone help with a bigger Meat task, but *that* can be the real time saver.

Take Care of Yourself

One of the best ways to beat stress is to take care of yourself. This includes eating right, exercising, and getting plenty of sleep. It also means making time for the after-work Desserts you enjoy, like spending time with family and friends, and pursuing hobbies. When school life gets hectic and you feel as though you haven't left the parking lot before sundown in a while, it's easy to let these Dessert tasks slide.

There will *always* be "one more thing" to do before you leave. At some point, you need to decide you are finished for the day and that you deserve to do something other than work.

Stop Worrying

One of the most important points to remember is that half the stress of getting it all done comes from *worrying* about getting it all done.

My mom has a great story she used to tell me when she caught me stressing out as a kid.

There are two cows and they are both faced with an immense pasture of grass to graze. The first cow stood in awe before it and said, "How in the world will I ever finish all this grass? There is surely far too much for me here." The second cow said nothing, and instead, put her head down, and started grazing.

In life, we want to be the second cow. By the time the first cow is finished worrying and actually begins the task, the second cow is already done, moved on, and ready to succeed in her next endeavor.

We have a habit of building up work in our minds to be far more awful than it really is. Why waste your time worrying about your overwhelming workload? Just start moving forward, one task at a time, and it probably won't take as long as you think.

Dealing with Criticism

Music teaching can be a very rewarding profession. Nothing matches that feeling after a great concert when your students worked so hard and absolutely nailed their performance.

However, teaching can also be a thankless job at times. Undue criticism from parents, students or administrators can make us feel unappreciated at best, and on the brink of quitting at worst.

When this happens, it's easy to lose our motivation to work at all. The lengthy to-do list on your desk seems suddenly meaningless. The temptation is to say, "heck with it, why bother?" However, these negative feelings do nothing but sap our energy. Learning to let go of that awful parent phone call or that harsh, uncalled for student comment takes practice.

"Don't Let Other People Make You Ugly"

A few hours before the Winter Concert, I was methodically moving through my pre-concert checklist: getting the stage set, programs folded, chairs set up, etc.

In the midst of it all, I saw my red voicemail light start blinking. No one ever wants to get a voicemail right before a concert. Odds are it was probably my best clarinet player's mother telling me she was throwing up and wouldn't be there tonight.

I reluctantly checked the voicemail, and was completely taken aback by what I heard.

As I suspected, it was a parent, but instead of reporting some sort of illness, she was berating my teaching abilities.

Mrs. Schwartz, I am appalled at the quality of trumpet you gave Timothy to use this semester. How dare you send my child home with such garbage. I'm in disbelief. My sister knows a lot about music and she says it looks like it hasn't been tuned in years. And the finish is coming off. I suppose we should just be thankful to have an instrument, but your negligence is unacceptable and I really don't want to even bring Timothy tonight.

I just sat there holding the receiver in my hand for a few moments. I was speechless. I knew I should be laughing (the trumpet hadn't been "tuned" in years? really?) but I felt extremely angry and hurt. Timothy was playing on a Conn trumpet I had borrowed from another school because he told me his family couldn't afford to rent one for him. I bent over backwards to beg and borrow instruments for my low-income students. Sure, this instrument was old, but it was a *great* horn. In fact, it was one of the best ones in my band room.

The more I sat there, the angrier I became. Her words swirled around in my head, growing more vicious and biting as I stewed.

I wanted to just go home. I tried to keep moving down my concert checklist, but I was so distracted I couldn't think straight.

"Who cares if these ungrateful parents have chairs to sit on at the concert?" I started to think to myself.

I wasted about half an hour of valuable concert prep before realizing I was allowing this angry parent to inhibit my productivity.

Then I remembered the advice my grandmother used to give me.

She would say, "Emily, don't let other people make you upset. Because when you get upset, it makes your face puffy, and that makes you ugly. You don't want to let other people make you ugly."

My grandmother is one of the feistiest and strongest people I know. I realized that if she had been with me in my classroom at that moment, she would have been angry with me for letting other people waste my time.

As music teachers, we are going to have phone calls and interactions that make us want to give up. Don't. It only hurts *us*. Let it roll off your back and keep going. (It might mean having an extra drink at Happy Hour, but that's a different story...)

In case you're wondering, Timothy did end up coming to the concert that night. I saw his mother standing in the back trying to avoid eye contact with me. I made a point to "bump into her" afterwards and give her a big smile and handshake as I told her what an excellent job Timothy did.

She mumbled something that sounded like "thanks" and quickly shuffled off into the crowd.

Victory.

Review

Controlling your stress level is a big part of time management.

1. Delegate. Trying to tackle everything yourself stresses you out and wastes your time. Allow others to help you.

2. Stop worrying. Half the stress of getting it all done comes from worrying about getting it all done.

3. Don't let others control your time. When parents and students upset you, don't take it personally or let it disrupt your productivity.

Remember, allowing your stress level to remain *fortissimo* is easy. Bringing it back down to a steady *mezzo forte* is difficult, but worth it.

8

TO BE EARLY IS TO BE ON TIME

"Jasmine, do you have your field trip permission slip today?"

"No...I haven't asked my mom yet. I will. The field trip isn't until next week."

Next Friday, I was taking the band to the local junior high to get a taste of what secondary music is like. The kids were so excited. They would be out of class for the whole day, meet the junior high director, play with his band, eat lunch, and learn how to enroll in band next year.

I had been nagging the students to turn in their permission slips and had everyone's except Jasmine's. Since the junior high was close enough to walk, and students were bringing their own sack lunches, it wasn't the end of the world if I didn't have a final headcount in advance. There were no buses or lunches to order. However, the students knew that I couldn't take them off campus during the school day without their signed permission slips.

"Jasmine, you realize that if I don't have your permission slip, you can't go on the trip," I reminded her again.

"I know Mrs. Schwartz. I'll get it to you. I've had a lot of homework this week."

I called home to Jasmine's mother that evening and asked if she had received the permission slip.

"Nope," she said. "I've heard about the field trip from other parents, but I'm not going to sign the slip until Jasmine asks me to. She only has good grades because I constantly remind her to do her homework. If she misses this field trip her grades won't suffer, she'll just be extremely disappointed. I think this might be the perfect opportunity to teach her some responsibility."

I was about to protest, but I stopped myself.

This wasn't a concert. No other student would be affected if Jasmine didn't go on the trip. It was just meant to be a fun and helpful trip for the band. In this case, I didn't feel it was my place to comment on her parenting strategy.

"OK, sounds like a plan!" I replied.

For the next few days, I diligently asked Jasmine each morning if she had her slip, and each morning it was the same excuse.

"I'll turn it in Mrs. Schwartz, oh my goodness."

Finally, the morning of the field trip came, and as expected, Jasmine came pounding on my door in tears.

"Mrs. Schwartz! My mom isn't answering her phone! I forgot to get her to sign the slip! I'm trying to see if she'll bring it to the school, but I keep getting the answering machine. I don't know what to do! I want to go on the field trip."

"Well Jasmine, that's a shame. I guess you can't come with us today," I said, hardly looking up from my computer.

Jasmine is a smart girl. She knew the rule and understood the consequence. She just sat in my room and cried for a few minutes.

Eventually, I went over to her and said, "Listen Jasmine, there will be other field trips, but you'll just have to miss this one. Next time I'm sure you'll remember to turn in your slip."

When her eyes dried up a bit, I sent her back to class just as the rest of the band was rushing in with their band shirts and sack lunches in tow.

As I was doing my final headcount, I began to feel terrible. I wondered if her mom and I had made the right decision. She was, after all, just 11 years old. Was that too young to be held 100% accountable for remembering things?

The field trip came and went. The students had a great time, and Jasmine got over her disappointment.

The next fall, I got an email from the junior high director.

Dear Emily,

I've been asked to pass a message along to you. We're going on a field trip next month, and Jasmine specifically asked me to call you and let you know that she was the first one to turn in her slip. She had her mom sign it after school and turned it in the same day I passed them out. She wouldn't let me take it until I promised her I'd tell you. She said it would make you happy.

Did it ever!

Strategy: Don't Wait Until the Last Minute

Music teachers constantly tell their students not to procrastinate. We say things like, "a lack of planning on your part does not constitute an emergency on my part," or "to be

early is to be on time and to be on time is to be late."
However, in our own lives, do we always follow our own
advice?

Teachers are known for two things:

1. Not following written directions

2. Procrastinating

I can't help you with the first one, but procrastination is
definitely a time management hurdle that you can overcome.

It's no surprise that music teachers are procrastinators. By
the end of the day, we are exhausted! We have a lot to do, but
we're so tired that we don't want to do it.

The problem with procrastinating is that it significantly
increases your stress level as the deadline approaches, and
you risk missing it altogether. This leads to more wasted time
trying to negotiate some sort of extension. Here are some
ways to avoid waiting until the last minute:

1) Use start dates

Sometimes we procrastinate not because we're tired, but
because we simply forgot! Setting a *start date* for every
deadline in your calendar is a great way to get things taken
care of early (see Chapter 5). A start date is a promise to
yourself you'll begin a task on a designated day. When you
say, "I'll do it later," you know exactly when "later" is.

2) Imagine the worst-case scenario

When we are on the verge of procrastinating, that little voice
inside us can come up with some pretty convincing
rationalizations. "It'll be fine!" we tell ourselves. "Nothing will
happen. You'll do it later and there won't be any problems."

We need to counter that voice with the *worst-case scenario.* What is the worst possible consequence of missing this deadline?

For example, if you miss a purchasing deadline, you might be unable to have new uniforms for next year. You could try calling the purchasing department and asking for an extension, but you know their deadlines are pretty strict.

The worst-case scenario would be standing in front of a roomful of students and parents and explaining to them that, while they sold bushels of candy, scrubbed dozens of cars on a Saturday afternoon, and stood over a hot griddle flipping pancakes, they would still not have their uniforms in time for the upcoming performance.

Then ask yourself, "Is that a risk I'm really willing to take?" Chances are, the answer is no.

3) Break your habits

If you procrastinate frequently, it has likely become a habit. Every time you wait until the last minute, luck is on your side, and everything goes off without a hitch, you convince yourself that procrastination isn't a problem. Whenever you turn in a form late, but someone covers for you, or you wait until the last minute to schedule an event, but people change their schedules for you, you become more and more convinced that things will just naturally work themselves out.

This causes chronic procrastinators to keep pushing their limits, waiting longer and longer to get started on those nagging little tasks. Eventually, of course, this all comes crashing down when something suddenly *does* go wrong and your safety net is not there. You swear this will never happen again, but by now, the procrastination habit is so ingrained that it's difficult to break.

If you know you tend to procrastinate, stop making excuses. Kick the procrastination habit *now* before it starts to have a more serious impact on your ability to get things done.

Break up Your Tasks

A procrastination habit becomes even worse when we put off big Meat tasks. We know this isn't smart, but when we're staring down a huge task on our list, it can be a little intimidating. We know it will be difficult, we know it will take a long time, and we know we don't have the time or energy at the moment to tackle something that monstrous. So we put it off until later.

Don't try to tackle huge tasks all at once. Instead, break them up into smaller chunks on your to-do list so you'll be more likely to actually complete them.

For example, let's say you teach AP Music Theory and have 60-70 tests to grade. If you saw "grade theory tests" on your to-do list, you're likely to think you don't have time for that and put it off. However, if you broke up that task into smaller chunks, and instead saw, "grade 20 theory tests" on your list, the task sounds much more manageable.

This concept reminds me of those little mini hamburgers you get as an "appetizer" at many restaurants these days. They call them "sliders." I hate those things! They are so delicious that I end up eating five or six of them because they are so tiny. I tend to forget they are adding up to quite a meal. You can harness that same concept for your time management. If you break up your huge Meat tasks into smaller pieces, pretty soon you'll have done more work than you even realize.

When you catch yourself about to put off a big task on your list, ask yourself, "What small piece of this task can I do *right now* that will make less work for me later?"

Create Your Own Deadlines

Some people protest that they *must* procrastinate because they work better up against the pressure of a deadline. I used to believe this was just a way of excusing procrastination, but I have since met many people who honestly do their best work when the pressure is on. If this is the case for you, you'll need to create your own deadlines.

When you receive a deadline to write in your teaching calendar, immediately make your own deadline two days earlier. Forget about the "real" deadline. Yours is now 48 hours sooner than everyone else's. This way, you can still work "under the gun," but you don't risk being late if an unexpected crisis or speed bump comes up along the way. It takes a little self-discipline, but creating your own deadlines can be a great first step towards ending your battle with procrastination.

Review

Procrastination is the enemy of successful time management. It's a nasty habit to break but it can be done by adhering to a few simple concepts.

1. Use start dates. Don't just say you'll do your work "later." Write down exactly *when* you plan to start.

2. Imagine the worst-case scenario. Just because things have always "worked out" in the past, doesn't mean they will now.

3. Break up your tasks. Don't let a big task on your to-do list intimidate you. Break it up into more manageable chunks and get started sooner.

As teachers, we should at least hold ourselves to the same standard to which we hold our students. If you expect *them* to be on time and proactive, then *you* should be too.

9

CIRCLE YOUR ACCIDENTALS

"F-sharp clarinets! First finger!" I hollered as I cut off the band.

The flutes rolled their eyes as they put their instruments down. I'm fairly certain that every other person in the band could pick up a clarinet and play a proper F-sharp at this point. We had stopped at this measure more times than I could count.

"Clarinets, every time we get to bar 45, you act as if that F-sharp surprises you. I can practically see it on your faces.

"The F-sharp was there when I passed this music out two months ago and I'm pretty sure it will still be there during the concert next week."

The voices of my college professors echoed in my head. "Never use sarcasm with the children."

Sigh. Maybe they meant, "Never use sarcasm...unless your students are clearly protesting accidentals?"

We isolated the section again, and of course, *now* they played it perfectly.

"OK everyone, let's start this from the beginning."

The band played wonderfully, until the brash sound of clashing half steps rang out at measure 45 as half the clarinet section continued to play an F-natural.

I didn't even have to stop the band this time.

"Oh my gosh, seriously?!" a trombone player called out from the back.

"Clarinets, can you please, *please* circle the accidental?"

"We *did* circle it, Mrs. Schwartz."

"Well, make a bigger circle!" one of the trumpet players shouted.

"Actually, the circle doesn't really help," said a quiet voice from the back of the clarinet section.

"By the time you see the circle, you've already played the wrong note, that's why I did it this way."

I went over and looked at her paper. Two lines before the accidental occurred, she had written something to herself in the margin.

Don't forget the F# is coming up.

"See? This way I remember to think about it before hand so I don't mess up."

We didn't begin playing again until each clarinet player had written the same sentence in his or her music. "If this works," I thought to myself, "I might just let the students direct the band."

We began the piece again. As measure 45 approached, I felt the suspense building in the room. All eyes were on the clarinet section. Would they do this right?

Yes. They would.

For the first time, every single clarinet player played the correct accidental and the melody finally sounded complete.

I tried to keep the piece going, but I couldn't because almost every member of the band stopped playing and erupted in applause.

I could tell this was going to be the end of the measure 45 saga.

Strategy: Anticipate Your Struggles

Just as some parts of a piece of music are going to be more difficult than others, some parts of the school year are going to be more hectic and more complicated as well. One thing I've noticed about teaching is that these stressful points come at the same time year after year. This means you know they are coming *and can anticipate them in advance.*

Don't be shocked when you feel as though you're going out of your mind with too much to do during the same few weeks of every school year. Just like my clarinet players had to anticipate their tricky accidental, you need to anticipate these stressful times and prepare for them accordingly.

My most stressful teaching times are the first week, the last week and concert weeks. Yours are probably similar. Because you know your to-do list is going to be extra long during those weeks, you can be constantly looking for things to take care of in advance in order to ease your burden during those crazy times.

Keep a Slow Day List

When you're in the heat of a stressful moment, it's easy to think of a million things you could have done sooner to prevent the panic. However, by the time it's all over, those things have vanished from your mind. This is why it's helpful to keep a Slow Day List.

When you're super busy, and catch yourself thinking, "Gosh, why didn't I do _____ earlier?" write it down on your list. Then, the next time you have a little down time, or a day that is slightly less busy than the rest, you can pull out the list and start knocking things off. Even if you're only able to accomplish *half* of the things on your Slow Day List, you'll be amazed at your reduced stress level when that hectic concert or festival week hits.

When I was growing up, one of my music teachers wrote each of her students a letter at the end of the year. The page-long letters were personalized, thanked us for our work, and acknowledged our special talents.

The letter meant so much to me at the time, and it means even more now, knowing how long it must have taken her to write all of them during the last hectic week of the school year.

I recently asked her how in the world she had found time to write all of them. She replied, "Well, for one thing, I certainly didn't wait until the end of the school year! I tried that once and it was an absolute disaster. Who in the world has time for that? I wrote them in February."

Ask for Help in Advance

When we are in the middle of that crazy week of the school year — that time when we barely have a moment to throw some food in our mouths around lunchtime, let alone finish anything on our to-do lists — we can't forget to seek help from others. The problem is, if we wait until we absolutely *need* help, it's often too late to ask for it. People are already busy or there is insufficient time to give them the training or resources they'll need.

Since you can anticipate when your busy times are likely to be, you can ask people in advance to assist you. For example, if you're a traveling teacher and have multiple performances on one day, you might ask someone at one of your schools — perhaps a custodian or fellow teacher — to help you set up. People are usually more than happy to pitch in when given enough notice.

Let them know a few weeks in advance and draw a diagram of exactly what you'll need. When you secure help in advance you'll be sure the task is done right, free up some of your valuable time, and most importantly, show that you respect other people's schedules.

Be Realistic

As you start crafting a lengthy to-do list for a hectic day, it's easy to lose track of how long things realistically will take to accomplish. You can't give yourself 90 minutes of tasks to do in only 30 minutes, and then stress when you don't have time to finish. Take a good look at the things you need to finish and set reasonable goals for yourself. You *will* get everything done, but you'll compound your stress if you expect to finish it all in an unrealistic amount of time. The longer you've been in your job, the easier it will be to judge how much time you'll need for specific tasks.

Review

You could probably look at your calendar right now and tell me which weeks are going to be the most stressful during the school year. Use that information to your advantage.

1. Anticipate your struggles. Prepare for your hectic times in advance.

2. Keep a Slow Day List. This way you'll remember which things you can finish earlier in order to ease your stress.

3. Ask for help in advance. We can't do everything ourselves, but we also can't cry for help at the last minute and hope to find it.

These stressful times are like the accidentals in our music. We know they are coming; we just have to be on heightened alert so we remember them before it's too late.

10

TEACHING IS A SYMPHONY, NOT A SOLO

In high school I spent many of my lunch periods either in the band room, or waiting outside for the director to open the door. On days that the room was closed, my friends and I were so angry! "What in the world could he possibly be doing? We want to go in and practice!" (Note that the word "practice" is used extremely loosely in this context and really means "hang out in the general vicinity of our instruments.")

Fast forward to my first few years as a teacher. My music room had a continuously open door. Students came in at break and lunch to practice, hang out, and help me organize things. I used lunchtime to hold extra sectionals. When non-band people dared to enter, I used the time to recruit new blood to the program. Even when the students didn't seem to be doing anything in particular, I didn't have the heart to kick them out because it was hot outside and I knew I wouldn't want to be on the playground either. (Reminder: I live and teach in Arizona where 100 degrees constitutes a "cool" day.)

I thought I was being a great teacher! However, I sensed myself becoming more and more isolated. As the months wore on, I couldn't understand why even though I loved the kids, I was beginning to hate my job.

One day, I was frantically making copies in the workroom between classes when a teacher stopped me.

"Aren't you the music teacher?" she asked me.

It took me a moment to respond. Was someone actually talking to me?

"Um, yeah." I replied. "I'm Emily. Nice to meet you."

"Hi Emily. I have such a soft spot in my heart for music. I played violin in the school orchestra all the way through high school and now my kids play too. How long have you been teaching?"

We talked for a few minutes about our teaching careers, and our own experiences in music. It turns out she had thought briefly about becoming a music teacher, but didn't think she was good enough to get a degree in music. She was also an avid hiker and told me about some of the local trails I should check out when the weather cooled down.

The conversation was brief but enjoyable.

On my drive home, I realized it was the highlight of my day. As I relayed this to my husband, I started to feel a little silly.

"Hi sweetie, I made a new friend at school today."

That sounded like something a 5-year-old would say. I knew something needed to change.

That week, I vowed to eat lunch with a person over the age of twelve each day. I had always told myself I "didn't have time" to take a lunch break, but starting now, I decided to *make* the time... to save my own sanity.

I sat down in the staff lounge, expecting a warm welcome, just like the one my new friend from the copy room had given me.

I was mistaken. Inside were three clusters of teachers, all sitting by grade level, discussing their own classrooms and curricula. I bravely sat down at one of the tables, introduced myself and set out to join the lively conversation.

I was met with some quizzical looks. After ten agonizingly long minutes, one of them stood up and left. The rest quickly followed.

Again, I felt like the 5-year-old that nobody wanted on the dodgeball team. Way to go, Emily.

I was frustrated, but persistent. I had made a promise to myself to eat lunch in there every day this week. After I had fulfilled that five-day commitment, I never had to set foot in the staff lounge again. And I wouldn't care!

The next few days were not unlike the first. I couldn't seem to "break in" to any of the cliques and left feeling irritated.

Finally, on the last day, I just sat alone at one of the tables, convinced it would be my last day in that horrid room.

Just then, a group of three giggly ladies came in. "Uh oh!" one of them said. "Looks like someone's at our table!"

I rolled my eyes and got up to move, but another member of the trio put her hand on my shoulder and said, "Oh goodness, we're just kidding! Welcome to the lunchroom! Why don't you eat with us?"

I found out during the course of our conversation that these ladies worked in the reading lab. They all had children of their own who were about my age, but that didn't seem to bother them. They asked where I was from and how I was adjusting to Arizona. Most importantly, *they didn't seem to want to talk about work!*

I had an extremely enjoyable lunch, and as we all got up to leave, one of the ladies asked, "So Emily, will we see you in here next week?"

"Absolutely."

Strategy: Don't Sacrifice Your Lunch Time

Music teaching can be a lonely profession. If you're not careful, it's possible to go for days with very little adult interaction. Sometimes, your brief lunch break is the only opportunity to cultivate and maintain adult relationships at your school. While it's tempting to work through lunch every day in an effort to be productive, that habit can lead to premature burnout. The short-term productivity gain is not worth the long-term consequences.

Remember, teaching is a symphony, not a solo. You need others to make your day enjoyable and effective. Your friendships at work are the Desserts of your Time Diet and it's important to schedule them into your day just as you would schedule any other obligation. Even if you only have lunch in the staff lounge twice a week, that time helps strengthen your connection to your school and your colleagues.

"I Hate the Staff Lounge"

Some teachers protest that the staff lounge is a toxic and negative place to be and that time spent there actually *increases* stress. I'll admit, at times I've felt that to be true, depending on the school. If your staff lounge is a breeding ground for complaining and gossip, seek out more positive places to dine. The P.E. office was always one of my favorite places to crash. Find out who the other "anti-staff-lounge" teachers are and seek them out.

"I Don't Get a Lunch Break"

If you are a traveling teacher, your "lunch break" might consist of devouring a peanut butter sandwich in your car while driving from one school to the next. This doesn't mean you must be doomed to a life of your colleagues thinking you're a substitute teacher. You'll just need to find other times to form these relationships. Try these ways of branching out:

1. Volunteer at the school carnival.

2. Participate in another organization's fundraiser.

3. Make an appearance at the staff holiday party.

4. Sign up for a committee that involves lots of teamwork.

5. Get to know the other teachers in your hallway.

All of these things take *time*, but it's important to think of them as investments in your healthy Time Diet. We'd all get more done if we worked nonstop, but we wouldn't be able to keep up that pace for long. Allowing time for relationship building makes working a more social experience, and it also builds your professional network. You never know when you might need each other!

The Students Aren't Your Friends

Remember, you can be friendly with the students, but they aren't your friends. This can be tricky, especially for new teachers who might be closer in age to their students than to the other teachers at the school. Make time to cultivate relationships with your colleagues. You can still provide your students with extra practice time and support without devoting every break and lunch period to them. That break during the day is there because you *need* it. Don't burn yourself out by never seeking non-student time.

Review

Your lunch time is important and shouldn't be first on the chopping block when you are faced with a long list of things to do.

1. Even if you choose to work through lunch some days, be sure to give yourself a break on other days.

2. Lunch may be the only social time you get. Take advantage of it so you don't become too detached from the rest of your school.

3. If the staff lounge isn't a place you like to be, find other ways to build relationships with your colleagues.

Remember, teaching is a symphony, not a solo. You won't find success in complete isolation.

Emily Schwartz

11

DECEPTIVE CADENCES ALWAYS RESOLVE

It was the first day of a new school year. As I poured myself a cup of peppermint mocha flavored coffee and headed out the door, a flurry of thoughts rushed through my head.

"Did my star trumpet player really move over the summer?"

"Would my new students be eager and ready-to-learn like last year's were?"

"Would there be a repeat of the great Band Room Ant Infestation of 2010?"

I'm sure I'm not the only teacher who wonders about things I can't control. If only students knew that teachers have "first day of school jitters" too, maybe they'd cut us some slack. (Probably not.)

As for the things I *could* control, I was feeling pretty good. I had made good use of the past week and the classrooms at my three schools were ready to go for the new year. Sure, there were a few lingering things to finish up, but I had more than enough time to do them. With a plan of attack for the day, I walked onto campus feeling very confident.

The first few classes went off without a hitch. Returning students checked out the same instruments as last year.

Incoming students listened in awe to my recruitment spiel. Eager children clamored to tell me about the fun things they did over the summer and to show off their new school clothes.

As 11:00 a.m. approached, I packed up my cart and prepared to repeat the entire morning at my next school. I was just about to follow my last class out the door when the principal's voice boomed over the loud speaker.

Attention students and staff. We are now going into a campus-wide lockdown. I wish I could tell you this was a drill. All I can tell you is that the situation is not on our campus. Please stand by for more information.

The students and I froze as we looked up at the loudspeaker. Unfortunately, with all of the horrible things that occur at schools these days, my first reaction when I hear "lockdown" is "shooter on campus." Thankfully, that did not appear to be the situation.

My *second* reaction when I hear "lockdown" is, "Exactly how long will I be trapped in this room with this group of students?"

If you've never experienced a lock down situation, I can tell you it's similar to a cage fight where only the strongest emerge at the end of the day.

I set my things back down on my desk and gathered the students for a rousing game of Music Bingo.

Once they started, I turned to Google to try to figure out what in the world was happening. As it turned out, there was an armed car jacking a few blocks from the school and the suspect was still at large. The police had put all schools on lockdown within a few-mile radius.

As it started to sink in that we were going to be here for a while, I looked down at my to-do list. How was I going to finish all of these things for my other school? Was I even going to *make it* to my other school today? What if we were stuck here for hours?

After about 45 minutes, the students started to get cranky and hungry. This was their usual lunchtime. When their complaining reached a peak level of annoyance, I finally said, "Look, we are all in this together. Sometimes things happen unexpectedly and we just have to roll with it and make the best of the situation."

Then it dawned on me that I was not following my own advice. I was so fixated on how this unexpected pitfall was disrupting my productivity that I wasn't even *trying* to figure out a way to make it better.

I looked at my to-do list again. I had to re-prioritize. The only things I truly *needed* to do that day were get the music ready for my afternoon classes and finish preparing the materials for the Back to School parent event. My students were eager to help me with these tasks and in exchange, I raffled off the "emergency" snacks in the first aid bin as well as a granola bar from my lunchbox.

After another hour or so, we finally received word that the lockdown was partially lifted. Students could now leave their classrooms, but police would stay at the school as a precaution until the end of the day.

I could hear the collective cheer resounding through the hallways. I think the teachers were cheering the loudest.

A police officer escorted me to my car. "You should be fine," she assured me. "Just remember, if you ever hear gun shots while you're driving, go faster. Every little bit of distance you put between you and the shooter makes you that much harder to hit."

Had I known I'd receive that advice today, I probably would have stayed at home. Where was my hazard pay?

I made it to my other school unscathed, just in time to see my last two afternoon classes and appear relatively calm and collected for the parents after school. The afternoon didn't go *exactly* as I'd hoped, but because I had adapted my productivity plan earlier, I was prepared enough to make it through.

And to think my biggest worry this morning was whether or not my first-day-of school lesson would be a hit with the students. I made a mental note to add, "Will I have to fear stray gunfire?" to next year's "first-day-worry-list."

Strategy: Be Flexible

No matter how well we plan our days, we are *always* going to encounter problems that have the potential to throw us off course. If it's not a first-day-of-school disaster, then it's a student discipline problem, a stolen instrument, an irate parent situation, or a last-minute meeting.

Rather than worry about how to prevent situations we can't control, or worse yet, use them as excuses for not accomplishing our work, we must learn to be flexible and adapt our plans to deal with these unexpected speed bumps that *will* come along.

Music wouldn't be nearly as interesting without a few deceptive cadences. When our teaching symphony throws us a V-vi instead of a V-I, don't panic. A pleasing resolution to tonic is still coming, it just might take a little longer to get there than you'd hoped.

There Are Many Paths to a Goal

If you are a planner at heart (like I am), you might find it difficult to accept that you can't control every moment of the day. If you have a detailed plan but hit a speed bump, there's no need to label the plan a total loss. Think of your whole to-do list as a goal and realize that there are many paths you can take to achieve it. If something disrupts your day and puts a roadblock in your path, just find another route.

When something goes wrong in your day, follow these steps:

1. Don't panic

Staying calm and keeping a clear head are essential to finding a workable solution to your problem. Getting angry just wastes valuable time and energy.

2. Utilize your resources

Finding a new productivity path might involve finding new ways to accomplish your tasks. Don't be afraid to ask people for help or to be a little creative in your efforts to get the job done.

3. Re-prioritize

When unexpected challenges are added to our day, we are forced to re-examine which tasks on our list are really important. Is it the end of the world if your curriculum presentation for parent night doesn't have a slide show?

4. Be sympathetic

Sometimes it isn't *our* day that's gone haywire, it's one of our colleagues' and we get called upon to help. While it's easy to become frustrated, remember that everyone has those days and yours will come around too. When a second grade teacher's father died a few days before state testing, I was amazed at how quickly her teammates each "adopted" seven children from her class so that the students would still have high quality instruction leading up to the test.

Things will *always* go wrong. Competitions will be rained out, buses will break down, and copiers will jam. Students will wait until they are about to walk on stage to trip and break their instruments. Parents will need to talk to you at the least convenient times. A to-do list that is set in stone has no place in the music classroom. We must be rigid enough to accomplish our goals while being flexible enough to handle the day-to-day madness of teaching.

Review

Teaching music is full of unexpected "adventures" during the day, but we can't let them derail our time management goals.

1. Find another way. When something unexpected arises, quickly adapt your plan.

2. Don't panic. If you let these curveballs stress you out, you won't be able to think clearly.

3. Be sympathetic. Unexpected emergencies happen to everyone. If you are quick to help others they will also be quick to help you.

Don't let a "deceptive cadence" ruin your day.

12

STRIVE FOR A STANDING OVATION

Ultimately, time management can be a bit of a misnomer. Sometimes it's not our *time* that needs managing, it's our *motivation*. After all, the key to mastering all of the strategies in this book is having the motivation to apply them.

If we are honest with ourselves, there are days when we *have* the time to do something, but we just don't want to! Either we are tired after a long day of teaching, or we've heard too many wrong notes for one afternoon, or the coffee machine was broken and we're desperately in need of some caffeine. Whatever the reason, there are some days when we would rather do *anything* but work.

Notice that those days are usually in the middle of the semester when nothing particularly exciting is happening and we start to feel stuck in a teaching rut.

It's easy to be motivated after your students just gave a wonderful performance where audience members just leapt to their feet, and you're reminded why you entered this business of music teaching in the first place. Since we can't have days like that all the time, we must harness that motivation and make it available to ourselves when we need it most. We must strive to make *every* day a "standing ovation" day.

Set Visible Goals

One of the quickest ways to lose motivation is to lose sight of why you are working so hard in the first place. This is why setting long-term goals is so important. It isn't enough to just have these goals in your head. It's essential to write them down and put them in a spot where you'll see them everyday. These can be personal goals, professional goals, or goals for your students. It doesn't matter.

I am currently working on my doctorate in music education. The degree consumes a huge chunk of my time and energy. After I'm tired from a long day of teaching, I still have three hours of graduate class in the evening and it's easy to lose my motivation. That's why I printed up a phony diploma that says, "PhD in Music Education presented to Dr. Emily Rose Schwartz" and hung it near my desk. Every time I see it, I'm reminded of why I'm working so hard and it gives me a little boost to keep going.

As music teachers, we all have those favorite students who inspire us. It's the "challenging" students who try our patience and truly test our abilities. Inside my desk, on a small slip of paper, I wrote, "Treat every student like your favorite student." That is my professional goal as a teacher: to inspire even the most difficult students to do their best and to treat them all fairly.

What are your goals? Why do you go to work every day? What are you trying to accomplish? Writing down the answers to these questions will not only help shape your path as a teacher, but motivate you to find the time to keep following that path.

The Drawer

Every teacher needs a drawer to collect all of the letters, pictures and trinkets students give us...that friendship bracelet a student made for you because you're her favorite teacher...that thank you note from a parent in appreciation of your hard work. They may not seem like much, but when you're having a frustrating day, they can be golden. We work much more quickly and efficiently when we are motivated, and a quick glance through The Drawer can be a great way to kick-start that motivation.

My Favorite Motivator

I wanted to leave you with one last story — one that sums up why education will forever be a part of my life — but it was hard to pick just one. Maybe I'd write about Amber, the star flute player from my first year of teaching, who was selected as the drum major of her high school band and couldn't wait to tell me because I had said she'd make a great leader one day. I could tell you about Dante, the clarinet player who gave me more attitude and behavior problems than any one teacher deserves and ultimately quit band only to show up at the last concert and tell me he just couldn't let me down.

The best kids and the "worst" kids tend to be the most memorable. However, my proudest teaching moment that continues to motivate me year after year, involved a very average student.

One summer, I was methodically going through each school instrument to prepare for the coming year. I removed any trash left in the cases, looked for repairs to be made, and removed old or broken reeds. I had finished with the trumpets and saxophones and was midway through the clarinets when something caught my eye.

A piece of paper was peeking out from behind the felt backing of one of the clarinet cases. When I pulled it out, I discovered that it was a neatly folded piece of notebook paper with the words "My Song, Don't Touch or Else" written in purple gel pen.

A rule-breaker by nature, I decided to open it and risk any horrible punishment that might befall me in the future. Inside was a scribbled melody on a hand-drawn staff. It was not very long, but it made use of quarter notes and eighth notes as well as accidentals and slurs. I wanted to cry.

This clarinet had belonged to Stacy McFarland, a very unremarkable band student. She was pretty bright, an OK player, and never really said much in class. She seemed to like band, but wasn't as enthralled with it as some of her classmates were. Normally, a student like this would gradually fade from the forefront of my memory as she slowly disappeared into the blur of all the other students I've taught.

However, something about band had lit a spark in her. I had not given her class any composition assignments that year. Nobody told her to go home and write a melody for her instrument. Something about her band experience inspired her to use knowledge she'd acquired in the classroom to create something that was her very own.

As music teachers, we may glorify our concerts. We may stress about festival ratings and obsess over ensemble enrollment. However, none of that matters if our students do not take something meaningful away from their experiences with music.

I thought about tracking down Stacy and returning her song, but I decided against it. I was never meant to find that song. That piece of paper wasn't about me, the band, or the school. It was about Stacy's love of music. I tucked it away in "The Drawer" and I look at it every time I need to be reminded why I love teaching music.

When our to-do lists seem endless, it's important to remember that we are not paper copiers. We are not equipment buyers or letter writers. We are not punishment givers, money collectors or event planners. Sure, we need to find the time to do all of those things, but that's only so we can be better at what we *really* are:

Soul nurturers

Creativity inspirers

Music messengers

Thank you for making a difference in the lives of children. The impact you make every day cannot simply be checked off a to-do list.

ABOUT THE AUTHOR

Praised for her dynamic energy, Emily Schwartz is a passionate music educator and speaker. Her teaching experience includes band, general music, and music technology at the kindergarten through university levels. Emily is also the founder of The Time Diet, a company dedicated to helping people find simple time management solutions. Her workshops have been lauded for their creative approach, engaging style, and most of all, their results. A Southern California native, Emily currently resides in Phoenix, Arizona with her husband Dan and her dogs Maggie and Molly where she is completing her PhD in Music Education at Arizona State University.

Emily Schwartz would love to offer a keynote or workshop at your next district in-service or state conference. Check out www.TheTimeDiet.org for more information
or email Emily@TheTimeDiet.org.

www.TheTimeDiet.org

Made in the USA
Middletown, DE
25 August 2015